IT'S OK NOT TO BE OK

A GUIDE TO WELL-BEING

Dr. TINA RAE

Illustrated by
JESSICA SMITH

STERLING CHILDREN'S BOOKS
New York

With love and thanks to Annie and
Connie—this is for you both.
– T.R

For everyone that needs to hear
that it's ok to not be okay, and to
everyone who has been there
for me through difficult times.
– J.S

This book is not intended as a substitute
for the advice of a healthcare professional.

STERLING CHILDREN'S BOOKS
New York

An Imprint of Sterling Publishing Co., Inc.
122 Fifth Avenue
New York, NY 10011

STERLING CHILDREN'S BOOKS and the distinctive
Sterling Children's Books logo are registered
trademarks of Sterling Publishing Co., Inc.

First Sterling edition published in 2020
©2020 Quarto Publishing plc

ISBN 978-1-4549-4278-8

Distributed in Canada by Sterling Publishing
Canadian Manda Group, 664 Annette Street,
Toronto, Ontario, Canada, M6S 2C8

For information about custom editions, special sales,
and premium and corporate purchases, please contact
Sterling Special Sales at 800-805-5489
or specialsales@sterlingpublishing.com.

Manufactured in China

Lot #:
2 4 6 8 10 9 7 5 3 1
12/20

www.sterlingpublishing.com

CONTENTS

HOW ARE YOU?

You've probably found yourself replying "fine," "good!", or "not too bad" when someone asks you how you're feeling. Often you will be feeling OK, and that's great—but what do you do on those occasions where you're not? Do you say so, or do you hide it?

If you're feeling good then "I'm OK" is a truthful response—but if you're not, and you are struggling a bit, not sharing or showing how you feel may not be so helpful. We all need to remember that **IT'S OK NOT TO BE OK**. What's not OK is when we hide our worries and stop looking after our mental health.

SO, WHAT DO WE MEAN WHEN WE TALK ABOUT MENTAL HEALTH?

If we think about looking after our bodies and keeping fit and well, it's easy to see how we also need to look after what's happening in our heads. Having good mental health means that we are generally able to think, feel, and react in ways that make us able to connect with other people and lead a healthy and generally happy life.

It's important to remember that we **ALL** have mental health, just as we all have physical health, and that there will be times when we find both difficult to manage. This is **NORMAL** and is part of being a human being. Whatever your experience, it's important to learn, think, and talk about mental health. You are not alone and don't need to feel ashamed or embarrassed about experiencing problems or struggling with your mental health.

In this book, we will explore some of the difficulties we might face including common mental health problems such as stress and anxiety, body image problems, and eating disorders. We will think about why these difficulties occur and the ways in which you can look after yourself so that they don't become overwhelming.

So let's get started, together.

TOP TIP

You may want to use a **NOTEBOOK** or **JOURNAL** as you read this book and write down any thoughts, feelings, questions, and discoveries as you go.

WHAT CAUSES MENTAL HEALTH PROBLEMS?

As we are all so different, there isn't one definite answer to this question.

But what we can say is that many people who experience problems may well have experienced situations, changes, and events that have made it harder for them to deal with life's ups and downs.

POSSIBLE CAUSES AND TRIGGERS

There are many different reasons why people develop mental health problems and they differ from person to person. Here are just a few:

BEING LONELY FOR LONG PERIODS OF TIME

LOSING SOMEONE YOU LOVE AND FEELING BEREAVED

BEING BULLIED OR STIGMATIZED

HAVING YOUR SELF-ESTEEM DAMAGED BY HURTFUL COMMENTS

BEING PHYSICALLY OR EMOTIONALLY ABUSED

MOVING TO A NEW SCHOOL

PARENTS SEPARATING

DEVELOPING A PHYSICAL HEALTH PROBLEM OR ILLNESS

EXPERIENCING POVERTY

During these times, it's especially important to check in with ourselves and keep track of how we feel. It's also important to reach out and ask for help early on, instead of waiting until we feel overwhelmed.

SIGNALS AND SIGNS

Your brain and body often send you signals and signs when it comes to mental health. Here are some things to be aware of that might suggest you are finding things difficult and are not feeling yourself:

HAVING TROUBLE CONCENTRATING

FEELING ANGRY

LOTS OF HEADACHES

NOT WANTING TO BE WITH FRIENDS

BEING AFRAID OF THE FUTURE

NOT SLEEPING WELL

THINKING NEGATIVELY

WORRYING ALL THE TIME

FEELING SAD ALL THE TIME

FEELING LONELY MOST OF THE TIME

FEELING TIRED ALL THE TIME

GETTING BREATHLESS

HEART RACING

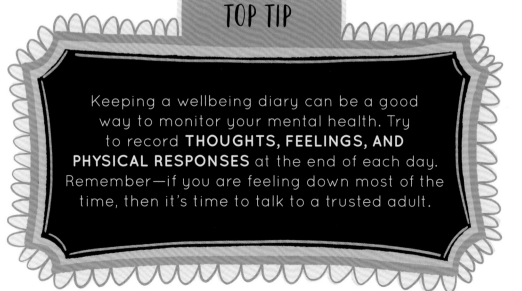

TOP TIP

Keeping a wellbeing diary can be a good way to monitor your mental health. Try to record **THOUGHTS, FEELINGS, AND PHYSICAL RESPONSES** at the end of each day. Remember—if you are feeling down most of the time, then it's time to talk to a trusted adult.

SELF-CARE

S elf-care is all about looking after yourself, taking some time for yourself, and doing something positive to boost and protect your mental and physical health.

~~~~~~~~~~~~~~~~~~~~~~~~

There are loads of ways to practice self-care. You don't have to be a yoga guru or a creative genius—it's all about finding something that works for you. You might even find that some of the things you already do each day count as self-care, but here are some activities to try if you need some inspiration:

• Journaling
• Spending time with pets
• Hanging out with friends
• Meditation
• Yoga
• Going for a bike ride
• Reading a book
• Playing an instrument
• Dancing
• Playing soccer with friends
• Watching films
• Listening to music
• Volunteering
• Growing plants.

As well as activities and hobbies, there are some things that we can and should ALL do to boost our self-care, such as:

• Keeping active
• Eating well and healthily
• Sleeping well
• Switching off from social media before bedtime
• Spending time with people who care for you and make a positive difference to how you feel
• Doing small acts of kindness for others
• Recognizing the rituals and routines that make you feel good
• Taking time to relax and giving your mind some time to switch off every day.

STOP, THINK, & REFLECT

Do you do any self-care activities already? What works for you?
Are there any activities you'd like to try?

ACTIVITY: SUPER STRENGTHS

IN ORDER TO MAKE THE MOST OF OUR POTENTIAL AND REMAIN POSITIVE AND WELL, WE NEED TO DEVELOP OUR STRENGTHS, AS WELL AS USING SELF-CARE STRATEGIES. THESE ARE THE THINGS THAT CAN HELP US TO COPE BETTER WHEN THINGS GO WRONG.

1. Take a few minutes of reflection to think about your strengths and the things you're good at. You could also ask a friend or family member to gather more ideas.

2. Write down these positive points so that you can use them in the future as a reminder of how amazing you are.

3. Consider how each of these strengths could help you to maintain your wellbeing and cope more effectively with difficulties.

4. If you feel comfortable, discuss your ideas with a trusted friend or adult. It can really help to share ideas and learn from each other.

EMOTIONS AND THE BRAIN

The brain is the most complex and mysterious part of our bodies. It's a built-in supercomputer, which gathers, processes, and sends information to our different organs. The brain also determines how we behave and what we say. It controls our complex thought processes, as well as OUR EMOTIONS AND FEELINGS.

THE POWER OF EMOTIONS

Emotions enable us to react to situations. For example, **ANGER** will set your heart racing, and **HAPPINESS** will make you smile. One of the key areas of your brain that deals with showing, recognizing, and controlling the body's reactions to emotions is called the limbic system. While the limbic system is made up of multiple parts of the brain, the center of emotional processing is the amygdala.

THE CHEMICAL FACTS

Emotions are controlled by the levels of different chemicals in your brain. Your brain adjusts how you respond to things and can alter your mood. If you're in danger, for example, your brain releases stress hormones, such as adrenaline, which make you react faster. We call this the **FLIGHT OR FIGHT** response. When danger subsides, your brain sends a signal and calming chemicals dampen the response of brain regions that create fear.

DID YOU KNOW? THE BRAIN IS SHAPED LIKE A WRINKLED WALNUT, BUT IF IT WAS UNRAVELED IT WOULD COVER APPROXIMATELY FOUR SHEETS OF PRINTER PAPER!

THE HAPPY CHEMICAL

Also known as "the happy chemical," serotonin contributes to wellbeing and happiness. However, sometimes the brain produces too much of the stress hormones and not enough of serotonin, which can cause of depression and anxiety. Doctors can prescribe medication called antidepressants to help, but we can all take practical steps and use natural tools to boost serotonin. For example:

- Exercising regularly
- Spending time in nature
- Eating foods rich in omega-3 fatty acids, such as fish, eggs, spinach, nuts, and seeds
- Using lavender oil on your pillow at night
- Practicing yoga, meditation, and mindfulness
- Reminding yourself of happy times
- Achieving goals you've set for yourself
- Doing something new or different.

STOP, THINK, & REFLECT

What could you choose from the list above to increase your happy chemicals?

HEALTHY BODY, HEALTHY MIND

We know that our bodies and minds are connected, so having a healthy body is just as important as having a healthy mind. If we look after our bodies, we will feel better about ourselves and produce more of the feel-good chemicals in our brains that make us feel happier every day.

EXERCISE

Exercise plays a big role in how well you feel and perform. But sports are not for everyone—you may be happier walking in the park or going to a dance class—the key is to find something that suits you and motivates you. **REMEMBER THAT WE DON'T ALL ENJOY THE SAME THINGS AND THAT IS OK.** It's important not to think of exercise as punishment—it's supposed to be enjoyable, as well as being good for you.

EVEN GOING FOR A 30-MINUTE WALK, FIVE TIMES A WEEK, CAN REALLY BOOST YOUR MIND AND BODY.

HEALTHY EATING

Having a balanced diet will help your body stay fit, both physically and mentally. Here are some key tips:

- Try to eat five portions of fruit and vegetables each day. Remember that a "portion" means the amount of food that fits in your hand.
- Your body also needs protein, carbohydrates, water, fiber, minerals, and fats.
- Salt and sugar can be unhealthy, but don't feel that you have to cut them out of your diet. The key is to eat them in moderation.

TOP TIP

To help fit in exercise around school, homework, and hobbies, it can help to plan out your own personal exercise routine. Try to find a balance between moderate intensity activities (such as jogging) and high intensity activities (such as soccer and gymnastics).

ACTIVITY:

ORANGE SEGMENTS

TRY THIS ACTIVITY TO RECORD YOUR CURRENT ACTIVITIES AND ALSO CONSIDER SOME NEW ONES.

1. Draw an outline of ten orange segments on a piece of paper.

2. Write down five things you do now to stay healthy (physically and mentally) in five of the segments.

3. Then use a different colored pen to record five new things in the remaining segments that you would like to do (and which are realistic) to stay physically and mentally healthy. Why not give some of them a try?

STRESS

Stress is a normal, necessary part of our daily lives. Each of us has an ideal stress level that allows us to function in an efficient and healthy way. If we don't get enough stress, we can become bored and lacking in energy. But if we have too much, we can become very troubled and upset and there can be a risk to our health.

It's important to remember that stress means different things to different people. For example, if you think about performing in front of an audience, some will find it difficult and become stressed, while others might enjoy the excitement and adrenaline rush.

THE STRESS BUCKET

Imagine that your head is a bucket, being filled with water, representing stress. Next, think about what would happen if the water kept coming, but you did nothing about it ... eventually your bucket would overflow.
To look after your head and avoid feeling overwhelmed, you need to make holes in your bucket to let the stress gradually drain away. Your "holes" might include things such as hobbies, relaxation, and spending time with friends. What things can you think of that work for you?

STRESS-BUSTING TIPS

- Try to identify what makes you feel stressed. Sometimes keeping a journal can help.

- Try to identify what it feels like when you are stressed. Draw it or write it down.

- Try to identify what calms you down and makes you feel good, and DO IT.

- Think about sharing this knowledge with friends, family, and teachers.

- Remember that lots of people feel stressed and anxious, but stress and anxiety can both be managed and treated.

- Don't suffer in silence. Think about who you could talk to or where you could go for help.

ACTIVITY: STEP OFF, STRESS!

IF YOU FEEL WORRIED ABOUT A SITUATION OR EVENT THAT'S COMING UP, WHY NOT GIVE THIS A TRY?

STEP 1
IMAGINE

the event in detail and focus on how you are most likely to feel.

STEP 2
PREPARE

for the event. For example, if you have a test coming up and there's a topic that you're unsure of, ask your teacher, friends, and family for help, or do more research yourself.

STEP 3
BE AWARE

of all the possibilities and outcomes of the event and imagine yourself being calm and relaxed in each one.

STEP 4
CHECK IN

before the event to make sure you have everything you need. For example, if you're giving a presentation and feel unsure of your script, have it written down on flashcards.

STEP 5
RELAX & UNWIND

before the event as well as afterward.

ANXIETY AND WORRY

As with stress, we all feel anxious sometimes—and that's OK! However, it's important to strike a balance and find ways to manage worry to avoid feeling overwhelmed.

WHAT IS ANXIETY?

Anxiety is a normal reaction to threat, which includes physical, emotional, and mental responses. For example, an increase in adrenaline, feelings of worry and confusion, thoughts about danger and imagining catastrophic outcomes. Normal levels of anxiety can help us to be more focused and motivated, and to solve problems more efficiently. But constant high levels of anxiety may mean that we experience constant physical feelings of panic, and we may try to avoid anything that might trigger anxiety, such as being alone, going to school, or talking in front of a group.

SYMPTOMS AND SIGNS

Worrying about things can make you feel anxious and you might notice some of these signs:

- **Increased heart rate**
- **Sweaty skin or going pale**
- **Feeling upset, on edge, angry, or irritable**
- **Feeling that something terrible is about to happen**
- **A dry throat or mouth**
- **Muscle aches or headaches**
- **Feeling tired or having little energy**
- **Poor digestion—stomach aches, bowel problems**
- **Concentration problems, mind racing**
- **Trouble sleeping.**

THE MORE ANXIOUS YOU GET, THE MORE YOU WORRY AND THE MORE ANXIOUS YOU BECOME AS A RESULT ... BUT THERE ARE THINGS WE CAN DO TO BREAK THIS CYCLE AND ALSO BEAT OUR WORRIES.

Here are some tips for beating your worries:

TIP 1—NOTICE! If you feel the signs of anxiety mentioned earlier, or you realize you are thinking negative thoughts, take note of these.

TIP 2—STOP! When you notice you are worrying, say to yourself "stop." Try thinking of something else, or doing something to keep your brain occupied, such as reading or baking.

TIP 3—GET AWAY. If things are worrying or upsetting you, try to get away—even if it's just for a minute.

TIP 4—WORRY TIME. Make time for five to ten minutes of "worry time" every day. If you find yourself worrying at a time when you have other things to do, tell yourself to stop, and think about it during your worry time instead.

TIP 5—SELF-TALK. If you keep worrying about the same thing, such as, "no one will like me at my new school," write down the opposite "positive" thought. For example, "people will like me. I'm a nice person." When you worry about the negative thought, tell yourself the positive thought.

REMEMBER TO SEEK HELP IF YOU FEEL YOUR ANXIETY IS BECOMING A PROBLEM AND TAKING OVER YOUR LIFE. YOUR DOCTOR CAN PROVIDE ADVICE AND MAY OFFER THE SUPPORT OF A COUNSELOR.

CHALLENGING NEGATIVE THOUGHTS

When we feel upset or under pressure, we tend to only look at the "bad" things, think in an extreme way, and take things personally. But it doesn't have to be this way—it's possible to challenge negative thoughts.

FAULTY THINKING

We all have negative thoughts, sometimes even on a daily basis, such as "she gave me a nasty look," "I can't do this work. I don't understand it," or "my hair looks bad today." But why do we have these automatic negative thoughts? They often arise from several errors in our thinking, including:

1. PUTTING OURSELVES DOWN—only focusing on the negatives and seeing bad things about ourselves.

2. EXAGGERATING OR CATASTROPHIZING—making things worse than they really are.

3. PREDICTING FAILURE—setting your mind ready to predict failure whatever the situation.

4. OVER-EMOTIONAL THOUGHTS—when your emotions overtake rational thought and stop you from thinking clearly.

5. BLAMING YOURSELF—thinking that everything that goes wrong is your own fault.

STOP, THINK, & REFLECT

Have you experienced these thinking errors before? When, where, and why? What might have helped you at the time?

WHAT WE BELIEVE ABOUT OURSELVES ISN'T ALWAYS TRUE. IT'S OFTEN NOT HOW OTHERS SEE US, AND WE NEED TO CHALLENGE THESE KINDS OF NEGATIVE BELIEFS.

ACTIVITY:
NO TO NEGATIVITY!

IF YOU FIND YOURSELF HAVING A NEGATIVE THOUGHT, ASK YOURSELF THE FOLLOWING QUESTIONS:

- What is the proof that my thought is true?

- What is the proof that my thought might not be true?

- What would my best friend say if they heard my thought? What would my teacher say? How about my parents or caregivers?

- What would I say to my best friend if they had the same thought?

- Am I making mistakes? For example, exaggerating, self-blaming, predicting failure, or assuming I know what others are thinking?

- How do you feel now? Do you still believe your thought is right?

BUILDING RESILIENCE

Resilience is about "bouncing back" from the things that life presents to us, even when they are hard. It is about being strong inside and able to adapt well to changes, challenges, and difficulties. It is also about "flourishing" in life, despite any problems or challenges we may face.

Taking risks and coping with challenges can feel like hard work but they are also good for us. We all need to learn how to manage challenges we face and not to be frightened of making mistakes. This is the key to resilience!

AM I RESILIENT?

Resilience is something that we can all learn so this is something to feel optimistic about!

If we are resilient we will have better health and we will feel happier. We are also less likely to develop emotional problems and mental health problems such as depression or anxiety.

STOP, THINK, & REFLECT

How well do you cope with problems? Are you able to bounce back and manage when things go wrong?

RESILIENCE TOOL KIT

Here are some skills and qualities that you can use to help you cope with challenges and build resilience:

- Humor—being able to laugh when things go wrong and see the funny side
- Inner direction—listening to the voice in our own heads
- Making good relationships
- Having a positive view of the future
- Perceptiveness—understanding what is really going on
- Independence—getting on with it on our own
- Flexibility—able to make changes

- A love of learning new things
- Feeling you can do things well
- Spirituality—feeling connected to something outside of us
- Being able to motivate yourself to get going
- Knowing who you are and why you think, feel, and behave in the ways you do
- Perseverance—to keep going when it gets tricky
- Creativity—to make or think up new and wonderful things.

Coping with change

Change is an inevitable part of life, but both positive and negative changes can be hard to deal with and accept. Here are some things you can do to make coping with change a little easier:

- Acknowledge that things are changing.
- Try to stick to your regular schedule.
- Exercise and try to eat as healthily as possible.
- Write down the positives that have come from the change and look for new opportunities.
- Ask for help.

MINDFULNESS

Being mindful means paying attention to the present moment, exactly as it is. Mindfulness can be a great way to ease anxiety, but it's also a great way to help everyone cope with the normal ups and downs of everyday life.

ACTIVITY:

MINDFUL MOMENT

MINDFULNESS IS ABOUT GETTING INTO A "MIND-FULL STATE." ONE OF THE SIMPLEST WAYS TO DO THIS IS TO STOP WHAT YOU ARE DOING AND TAKE A MINUTE TO FOCUS ON YOUR BREATHING.

1. Sit down somewhere quiet and close your eyes.

2. Direct your attention to the sensation of each breath in...
... and each breath out...

3. Become aware of the feeling of air as it enters and then leaves your mouth or nostrils.

4. Thoughts will enter your mind. Become aware of them, note them without judgment, then let them pass. Imagine pinning your passing thoughts to a drifting cloud or a leaf that floats away down a river.

5. Focus your attention on your breath. In and out, in and out...

6. Slowly open your eyes.

ACTIVITY: THREE SENSES

THIS ACTIVITY HELPS YOU TO NOTICE WHAT YOU ARE EXPERIENCING RIGHT NOW THROUGH THREE SENSES—SOUND, SIGHT, AND TOUCH. THINK OF YOUR ANSWERS SLOWLY, ONE SENSE AT A TIME. IT'S IMPOSSIBLE TO DO THIS EXERCISE AND NOT BE MINDFUL! ASK YOURSELF:

• What are three things I can **HEAR**?

a car going by

the clock on my wall

music in the next room

• What are three things I can **SEE**?

a table

a sign

a person

• What are three things I can **FEEL**?

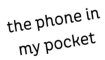

the phone in my pocket

the chair under me

the floor under my feet

RELAXATION

Let's face it: life can be stressful. There's so much going on, so many things to see and do—there can be a lot of pressure. So, it's important to give yourself a break from time to time. Take some time out—
YOU DESERVE IT!

ANXIETY VS. RELAXATION

Being relaxed is the opposite of being anxious, right? It might sound obvious, but have you ever stopped to think about what's going on inside your body and mind during these different times? Look at the two lists—one shows what it can feel like to be anxious, while the other shows what it can feel like to be relaxed:

Cross, jumpy	Happy, calm
Heart beating fast	Heart beating slowly
Breathing fast	Breathing slow and easy
Skin pale or sweaty	Skin normal, not sweaty
Muscles trembling	Muscles relaxed
Stomachache or headache	No stomachache or headache
Thoughts racing	Thoughts normal

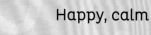

To avoid anxiety, you might think that you should always be relaxed. But no one can be relaxed all the time! We all need to find the right balance and have enough "downtime" so that we can manage the anxious moments when they happen to us.

ACTIVITY: RELAXATION REVELATIONS

GIVE IT A TRY! CHECK OUT SOME OF THESE SIMPLE RELAXATION STRATEGIES.

Breathe

Breathe in and out regularly and count in your head while you breathe. Breathe in for three, out for three...

Relax your muscles

Tense your muscles and then let them go floppy and relaxed. Include all your muscles, even those in your face, back, and stomach.

Picture a relaxing place

Create an image in your head or draw your relaxing location on some paper.

Stretch

Stretch your arms over your head, reaching for the sky; shrug your shoulders tight into your neck and curl up into a ball, as if you are a tortoise hiding in its shell; wrinkle your nose as if you are trying to get a bug off it; clench your jaw... and then release.

Imagine and use your senses

Imagine it has been raining and you are standing barefoot in mud. Then, visualize yourself squishing your toes in the mud—wriggle your toes. How does it feel?

TOP TIP

Why not try keeping a **RELAXATION DIARY**? Each day, record what you did to relax, and how it made you feel. Review this every week to find the **BEST BALANCE** for you.

POSITIVE
MENTAL ATTITUDE

It's not always easy to be positive and to think about what is good about ourselves and our lives. We know that our negative thinking can get in the way but developing a positive mental attitude can really help.

MAKING A START

We can train ourselves to be more positive and to act in more positive ways. Doing so can increase our happiness and decrease stress levels. The aim is to be hopeful, brave, and to find the good in things. Here are some steps to take:

1. Recognize that change is needed.

2. Believe change is possible.

3. Let go of negative feelings and past experiences.

4. Stop criticizing yourself.

5. Be mindful and focus on the present moment.

6. Have a positive vision for your future.

ACTIVITY:
SELF-LOVE STICKY NOTES

If we think positively about ourselves, we feel positive. This is how self-love works and what you tell yourself is powerful. Here are examples of things you could tell yourself to practice positivity:

Use sticky notes or scraps of paper to write down positive statements every day. You could even stick them around your bedroom and create a whole wall of positivity.

SUPER SKILLS

Here are some key skills needed for a positive mental attitude:

FOCUS

People who think positively are more likely to remain focused on a task because they are not distracted by worrying about other problems. Try to focus on each task at hand —you will feel more productive, more in control, and happier as a result.

FLEXIBILITY

You need to know that failure and making mistakes is part of learning. It is not a bad thing. You need to keep going and not give up—even in the tough times.

CREATING HAPPY CONNECTIONS

Surround yourself with others who are positive and care about you. It is important to avoid those who pull us down and make us feel as if they have sucked our energy from us.

SELF-BELIEF

As simple as it sounds, sometimes people become successful simply because they believe in themselves. Positive thinking breeds confidence, and confidence is one of the major building blocks of success.

27

SOCIAL MEDIA

Be honest ... how much time do you spend checking your phone? And how much of that time is spent on social media? Social media can help us to feel connected with friends, but spending too much time on it can negatively affect our wellbeing.

~~~~~~~~~~~~~~~~~~~~~~

There are three main issues to think about:

1. SLEEP—if you're constantly checking your phone and don't switch it off at night then you won't sleep as well as you should. This can then lead to feeling down, depressed, and anxious.

2. THE "LIKE" PROBLEM—chasing "likes" can make us feel insecure and doubt our self-worth. If we post stuff online, we put ourselves at risk of receiving negative and mean comments as well as compliments or praise.

IT'S POSSIBLE TO BECOME ADDICTED TO SOCIAL MEDIA. SOCIAL MEDIA SITES ARE DESIGNED TO DRAW PEOPLE INTO THEM AND CHECKING THEM CAN BECOME A COMPULSIVE ACTIVITY.

3. SOCIAL COMPARISONS—

if we look at other people's pictures and lives and compare them to our own, this can make us feel jealous and anxious. It can seem like others are happier or having a better time than we are and this can make us feel like we cannot measure up, that we're missing out or not part of the "in group." Browsing social media when you're feeling sad or lonely can actually make you feel worse.

DID YOU KNOW? A WHOPPING 80% OF TEENAGERS USE SNAPCHAT AT LEAST ONCE A MONTH.

TOP TIP

Don't forget that used in the right way, social media can be really positive: you can keep in touch with friends, post things to make others feel better about themselves, and share good advice. However, it's important to make sure the accounts you follow online are those committed to bringing about positive change.

STOP, THINK, & REFLECT

When does social media make you feel happy? Does it ever make you feel anxious? Would it help to take a digital detox and reduce your screen time?

KEEPING SAFE
ONLINE

There are a huge amount of things to see and do online that can help boost our mental health. But it's important to know how to navigate and keep safe online. It's all about being aware and being responsible.

TEN ESSENTIAL RULES

1) Don't post personal information online—like your address, email address, or mobile number.

2) Think carefully before posting pictures or videos of yourself. Once you've put a picture online most people can see it and may be able to download it. It's also not just yours anymore, and it will remain in cyberspace forever, even if you delete it.

3) Keep your privacy settings as high as possible.

4) Never give out your passwords.

5) Don't befriend people you don't know.

6) Don't meet up with people you've met online. Speak to your parent or guardian about people suggesting you do.

7) Remember that not everyone online is who they say they are.

8) Think carefully about what you say before you post something online.

9) Respect other people's views. Even if you don't agree with someone else's views, you don't need to be rude or unkind.

10) If you see something online that makes you feel uncomfortable, unsafe, or worried: leave the website, turn off your computer, and tell a trusted adult immediately.

ONES TO WATCH

As well as unlocking a wonderful world of filters, friends, and emojis, being online means that you're opening up the possibility of coming across these serious issues:

1. BULLYING—be sure to tell a trusted adult if you feel you are being bullied. Block the number on your phone and change your number. If the problem is serious you can report it to the police, cyber mentors, or your school.

2. SEXTING—sending sexual images is dangerous and puts you at risk of abuse. Don't go there and, if asked, tell a trusted adult immediately.

3. PORNOGRAPHY—be careful to avoid anything pornographic online. Report it at once and do not feel ashamed or embarrassed. Adults know children are likely to have seen pornography online for the first time accidentally (e.g. via pop-ups or shown by someone else unexpectedly).

TOP TIP

Keep talking to trusted friends and adults about what you are doing and seeing online. It's always a good idea to share your accounts with your parents. Don't be afraid to discuss any issues or things that you feel uncomfortable or worried about—hiding your worries will only increase anxiety.

BODY IMAGE

What do you see when you look in the mirror? Having a positive body image is not as simple as just thinking you look amazing!

Seeing body images of celebrities and models can reduce self-esteem and increase anxiety. The media puts pressure on us and often suggests that we should look a certain way. But the truth is that THE PERFECT BODY DOESN'T EXIST.

> **EVERY BODY IS A GOOD BODY:**
> Human beings come in many shapes and sizes...
> ...we all have different physical characteristics and abilities...
> ...and these differences should be respected and valued—
> they are what make us UNIQUE.

POSITIVE BODY IMAGE

It's so important to respect your body. You might think or have been told that you're "different" but you are YOU and that's OK. Having a positive body image means:

- Being happy with your body the way it is

- Feeling comfortable with your body

- Feeling satisfied with how you look

- Choosing to focus on your good parts and strengths instead of things you feel are not so good

- Recognizing that who you are as a person is more important than how you look

- Knowing that the health of your body is more important than how it looks

- Appreciating your body for what it can do

- Viewing a range of weights, shapes, and appearances as beautiful.

STOP, THINK, & REFLECT

Do you think you have a positive body image?
What do you need to work on to improve it?

ACTIVITY:
BODY HABITS

TRY OUT THESE ACTIVITIES AND BEGIN TO SEE HOW YOU CAN DEVELOP SOME HABITS WHICH MAKE YOU FEEL HAPPIER, MORE CONFIDENT, AND INCREASE YOUR SELF-ESTEEM.

My healthy body
What makes a body healthy? Think of as many things as you can, such as eating well, exercise, etc. Make a list and tick those that you already do.

My body can do...
Your body is not just something to be looked at and admired—it also allows you to breathe, move, sleep, and live a healthy and happy life. What does your body do for you? Draw a self-portrait and write your ideas around it.

Bad body habits
Bad body habits are not good for us—physically or mentally. Write a list of habits that may be bad for our bodies, such as eating junk food, dieting, not exercising, exercising too much, etc. Try to identify what the equivalent good body habit would be for each.

My daily dose
Think of a range of healthy habits that you could do on a daily basis. What does this look like? What have you included and why?

PROBLEM SOLVING

We deal with problems almost every day. Minor problems can often be solved by thinking of a simple solution on the spot or using a strategy that worked in the past. But problems that don't go away can affect our wellbeing. Left unsolved, a small problem can become a big problem and leave you feeling frustrated, stressed, and hopeless. Developing problem-solving skills can help you deal more effectively with stress. These skills can also boost your happiness, self-esteem, relationships, and performance at school.

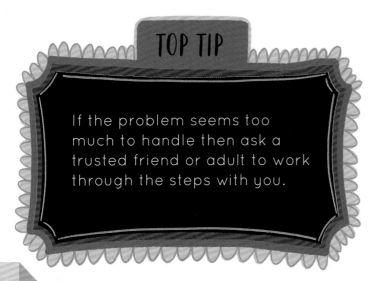

TOP TIP

If the problem seems too much to handle then ask a trusted friend or adult to work through the steps with you.

PROBLEM SOLVING STEPS

Solving problems step-by-step rather than head-on can help reduce anxiety. Here are some key steps to take when you come across a problem:

1. Write down what the problem is. Be specific: "I'm worried I won't cope" isn't specific, but "I'm worried I'll forget people's names when I go to my new school" is.

2. Next, think about the possible solutions to the problem. Write them down.

3. Go through the solutions one by one and think about the possible consequences each of them might have. Then, write down the pros and the cons of the solutions.

4. Consider the pros and cons, then choose a solution. If you can, ask someone else you trust whether they think this is a good solution. Then go and do it!

5. Finally, review your progress. Is the problem still there? Has it changed? Repeat the steps and problem solve again if you need to.

Facing fears

In order to manage our fears, it can help to have "give it a try" behaviors. This doesn't mean that if you're afraid of heights you should go straight up the highest building you can find. It's about taking things slowly, tackling the problem gradually, and recognizing that fears are not necessarily there forever—we can do something about them.

ANXIETY LADDER

1. Draw a ladder with 6 steps and write your goal on the top step.

2. Think of all the steps you could take to face your fear and reach your goal. For example, if you're afraid of dogs, steps might include looking at a picture of a dog, watching a video of a dog, listening to a dog bark, being in the same room as a dog, stroking a dog, etc.

3. Give each step a rating from 1 to 5, with 5 being the scariest.

4. On the bottom step, write one of your "1"s, on the second step, a "2," a "3" on the third step, a "4" on the fourth, and finally a "5" on the penultimate step.

5. Begin at the bottom of the ladder and try the task on the first step. Once you've managed it and feel comfortable, try the next step. The idea is to build up slowly, noticing and celebrating every step of the way until you reach the top of your ladder.

EATING DISORDERS

Eating disorders cause unhealthy actions and attitudes toward food. Many children and young people have difficulties with their eating styles and sometimes these can become very serious. It is important to understand more about these difficulties and how to recognize if you or a friend have a problem.

For some, dieting, overeating, bingeing, and purging may begin as a way to cope with difficulties and to feel in control, but these are very unhealthy and dangerous behaviors. Over time, eating disorders can damage physical health, mental health, and self-esteem. Recognizing them and getting help as soon as possible is key.

WHAT CAUSES EATING DISORDERS?

Eating disorders can be really complicated and there isn't always a single cause. Sometimes they occur because:

• Losing weight might make a person feel in control.

• A person is unhappy or suffering from mental health conditions such as depression and anxiety.

• The media idealizes being thin and suggests that we should look a certain way.

• Some people use eating disorders to cope with painful emotions and low self-esteem.

• Puberty can trigger disorders such as anorexia, which reverses some of the physical changes of puberty and therefore delays some of the challenges of becoming an adult.

EATING DISORDERS ARE SERIOUS ILLNESSES, BUT WITH THE RIGHT TREATMENT PEOPLE CAN, AND DO, RECOVER.

Have you ever thought you needed to stop eating to lose weight, or eaten too much because you felt lonely or unhappy? If so, then you are not alone. It's OK and good to admit it instead of hiding it. If you are worried you could:

1. Read up on eating disorders and speak to people you trust.

2. Read some real-life stories to see how other people have coped.

3. Try to be honest with yourself and those close to you about what you are, or are not, eating.

4. Keep a diary of what you eat. Make a note of how you feel when you do, and do not eat, to help see if there are any connections.

5. Don't punish yourself or give yourself a hard time about how much you eat or how much you weigh.

6. Don't linger in front of the mirror.

7. Talk about it with friends and family.

8. Ask for help from your doctor. Your doctor may refer you to a specialist counselor, psychiatrist, or psychologist.

DEPRESSION

We are all unhappy from time to time, but depression is a serious mood disorder where people experience lasting feelings of unhappiness and hopelessness. It's OK not to be OK, but it is NOT OK to feel this way all of the time.

SYMPTOMS AND SIGNS

Depression isn't the same as stress or anxiety. People will often say "I'm stressed" when what they really mean is "I'm feeling down, sad, or fed up." Here are some signs that could suggest a person might be depressed:

- Low mood most of the day, nearly every day
- No interest in things
- Changes in weight and/or appetite
- Slower thinking and movement
- Loss of energy
- Feeling tired all the time
- Feeling worthless
- Lack of concentration
- Irritability
- Freezing others out
- Morbid or potentially suicidal thoughts.

Sad events

By the end of elementary school, most children will have experienced a life challenge of some kind, e.g. the death of a pet, a loved one dying, or parents separating. Feeling low and sad after such events is normal and doesn't automatically mean you are depressed. During these times, remember to check in with yourself and talk to trusted adults about your feelings if you can.

Here are some things to try if you find yourself feeling low:

- Talk about your feelings with a teacher, counselor, or mentor who will listen without judgment.

- Use creativity to process emotions. Drawing, painting, and dancing are great ways to express how you feel.

- Accept that sadness is normal and that everyone feels blue from time to time.

- Remember that you have felt sad in the past and that those feelings went away.

- Keep doing the things you enjoy and keep seeing the people you enjoy spending time with.

- Use exercise as a natural antidepressant: it produces endorphins, the natural "happy hormones" of the brain.

- Challenge your negative thoughts (see pages 26-27).

Asking for help

Depression isn't always obvious to others. Telling someone to "pull yourself together," "it's nothing to worry about," or "it's just the January blues" can be really unhelpful if your unhappiness is actually more serious than it may seem on the surface. If you are feeling depressed and someone tells you to snap out of it, tell them that it's not that simple and that you need help. Do not let them dismiss your feelings of unhappiness and remember that you don't have to suffer in silence.

ADHD

ADHD (Attention Deficit Hyperactivity Disorder) is a mental health condition that causes people to have a lot of energy. People who have ADHD often find it hard to concentrate and may struggle to control what they say and do.

WHAT DOES ADHD LOOK LIKE?

Someone with ADHD might be:

- **Inattentive**—unable to concentrate for very long or unable to finish a task

- **Disorganized**—often losing things

- Easily **distracted and forgetful**—unable to listen when people are talking

- **Hyperactive**—fidgety, unable to sit still, and restless

- **Noisy**—talking constantly and struggling to do "quiet" activities

- **Impulsive**—speaking without thinking about the consequences, interrupting, and unable to wait or take turns.

If you experience any of these symptoms, it doesn't mean you definitely have ADHD. But if any of them are making your everyday life difficult and you are finding it hard to focus in class then it's a good idea to ask for help from your GP or a school psychologist.

HAVING ADHD DOESN'T MAKE YOU A BAD PERSON! IT SIMPLY MEANS YOU AND YOUR TEACHERS WILL HAVE TO WORK HARDER TO HELP YOU CONCENTRATE AND FOCUS IN CLASS.

STOP, THINK, & REFLECT

What helps you to concentrate? What makes it more difficult? Make a list of what works and what doesn't work for you. You might then want to ask your teacher, mentor, or a family member to help you think more about what could be done differently to help you improve your skills.

Concentration and focus

There are lots of simple and effective things we can all do to get better at concentrating and remaining focused. Here are some tips for doing so at school:

What you can do:

- Make to-do lists and tick things off as you go.
- Set realistic goals—don't make them too big or ambitious!
- Split big tasks into small stages.
- Before you start an activity, make sure you have everything you need.
- Use a timer when doing a task to help you concentrate and stick to it.
- Ask your teacher for activity breaks—give yourself a chance to move and breathe to help you refocus afterward.
- Use mindfulness to unwind and chill at the end of a task.

What your teachers can do:

- Aim to make directions as clear as possible.
- Reduce the noise and distractions.
- Help you find a quiet seating space.
- Check in with you regularly.
- Give rewards and change them regularly to encourage motivation.
- Set up a buddy system for you.

PERFECTIONISM

A perfectionist is a person who strives for flawlessness and refuses to accept anything short of perfection. Wanting to do well in life can be a positive motivation but obsessing about being perfect in all you do can hold you back and have a negative impact.

SO WHAT DOES PERFECTIONISM LOOK LIKE?

Here are some common signs:

- Refusing to try new things in order to avoid making mistakes.

- Taking a long time to complete something because you are checking for mistakes and starting again if you find one.

- Setting yourself excessively high performance standards.

- Being overly critical of yourself.

- Putting off things that look too hard to do.

- Giving up and getting upset when you can't do something.

- Asking for help before you try something.

- Thinking that your work is never good enough.

IS IT A BAD THING?

There's nothing wrong with aiming high, but constant perfectionism can become a bit of a burden. Perfectionism is something to watch out for as it can develop into anxiety problems and low self-esteem. It can also make you feel physically unwell and you may have headaches and feel a lot of tension in your body. If you try to be perfect all the time this may make you feel unhappy and you may find it difficult to cope with schoolwork and with friendships. Try to be open and honest as soon as you think this is a problem for you and talk to an adult. We can all change our behavior—being brave enough to try is often the hardest part!

TOP TIPS

If you feel that you're trying to be perfect and fear making mistakes:

• Try to focus on being brave rather than being right, smart, or excellent.

• Think about failure as a chance to learn something—we can all learn from our mistakes.

• Rather than give up, be brave and tell yourself: "It's OK! I just can't do this YET!"

• Talk about your fears with an adult or friend.

• Don't use self-blame language such as "It's all my fault" or "I'm useless".

• Be kind to yourself. Tell yourself: "I made a mistake. That's ok. I'll get it next time."

• Use mindfulness, remember to relax, and make time for fun!

• Make a list of the advantages and disadvantages of trying to be perfect.

OBSESSIVE COMPULSIVE DISORDER

Obsessive compulsive disorder, also known as OCD, is an anxiety disorder which causes a person to have frequent and obsessive thoughts that can sometimes be negative. Often sufferers try to control these thoughts by compulsively repeating an action, which can provide some relief from the thought-process.

Bad thoughts might include:

Worrying that something terrible will happen

Thinking you're dirty or smelly, or you're going to get sick

Worrying you're going to hurt other people

Convincing yourself that something horrible will happen to the people you love

Worrying that you'll lose control.

WHAT DOES OCD LOOK LIKE?

Here are some common signs and habits:

• Constantly and repeatedly checking things, sometimes for a "magical" number of times.

• Rearranging your things until they feel "just right."

• Excessively cleaning yourself or your surroundings.

• Repeating mental rituals in your head to try to get rid of a bad thought.

• Avoiding any situation where you feel you may lose control of yourself, or get dirty, or catch something.

• Constantly looking for help from others (e.g. asking "Did I do anything wrong?", "Are you sure?").

WHEN TO ASK FOR HELP

If you feel that you are repeating behaviors obsessively to try to cope, then you should talk to a trusted adult. In particular, see your doctor so that you can get the right help, if your repetitive behaviors:

• Take up a LOT of your time—at least an hour every day.

• Completely interfere with your life, your friendships, and going to school.

• Are causing you huge anxiety, stress, and unrest.

TOP TIPS

1. Don't push scary thoughts away as they will just come back stronger.

2. Remember that scary thoughts are not dangerous, they are just thoughts.

3. Think about the OCD as a monster—don't feed it by giving in to the fear.

KINDNESS

IF WE DO GOOD, WE FEEL GOOD!

Kindness is very powerful—doing kind things for others can make them feel happy, but did you know that these acts of kindness can also make you feel happier and more positive about yourself? Kindness is good for everyone's mental health— it matters!

There are so many ways we can be kind and think of others. We can volunteer, tutor, and help people through hard times. But it's not all about grand gestures—we can also be kind in very simple ways, such as smiling at someone, holding the door open, or giving a compliment.

Positive psychology

It is the study of what makes us human beings strong and happy, and how to be our "best selves." It's key to helping us to have good mental health and leading happier and more meaningful lives. Through research, positive psychologists have shown us that practicing kindness and gratitude can help us to feel happy.

TOP TIP

Try to plan three kind acts every day. The little things really do count—sending a nice message, helping out or making a small gift are all great ways to make others feel happy and loved.

GRATITUDE

Being grateful is about much more than just saying thank you—it's about not taking things for granted and having a sense of appreciation and thankfulness for life.

Taking time to be grateful is not about ignoring the bad things—it helps us focus our attention more on the positive, rather than just thinking about the negatives. As a result, people who are grateful tend to be happier, healthier, and more fulfilled. Being grateful can also help people cope better with stress.

EVEN ON A BAD DAY THERE ARE USUALLY SOME THINGS THAT WE CAN FEEL GOOD ABOUT!

ACTIVITIES

TRY THESE ACTIVITIES AND SEE WHAT DIFFERENCE THEY MAKE TO YOUR HAPPINESS LEVELS.

1. Three good things

At the end of each day, write down three good things that happened and why you feel thankful. Read them to yourself before you go to sleep and then again, the next morning.

2. Letter of thanks

Write a letter to say thank you to someone who had been kind to you or someone that you love. Tell them why you are grateful.

3. Moment of appreciation

Make a list of things you do each day that you are grateful for (e.g. having clothes to wear, tasty food to eat, great friends to hang out with, etc.).

BULLYING

Bullying is when a person or group deliberately tries to make someone else feel upset, scared, or ashamed. Bullying can make a person feel isolated, worthless, lonely, scared, angry, and insecure. It can also lead to more serious mental health problems like depression and anxiety.

~~~~~~~~~~~~~~~~~~~~~~~~

WHY DO PEOPLE BULLY?

There are four main types of bullying: physical, verbal, psychological, and cyber (online) bullying. Lack of self-esteem, anger, family issues, stress, and trauma are among reasons why people bully others. Sadly, hurting other people is often the only way they have to feel better about themselves. Sometimes people bully because they are being bullied themselves.

REMEMBER THAT EVERYONE HAS THE RIGHT TO BE TREATED FAIRLY AND RESPECTFULLY.

WHAT SHOULD YOU DO IF YOU ARE BEING BULLIED?

• **BUDDY UP** with a friend on the bus, in the corridors, or at break time, etc. to avoid being alone with the bully.

• **TALK TO SOMEONE** you trust, such as a friend, sibling, counselor, or learning mentor. They may offer some helpful suggestions and it may help you feel a little less alone.

• **HOLD THE ANGER**—it's natural to get upset by the bully, but that's what bullies thrive on—it makes them feel more powerful. Instead of reacting, try taking deep breaths, counting to ten, or later, writing down your angry words instead of saying them.

• **ACT BRAVE AND IGNORE THE BULLY.** Firmly and clearly tell the bully to stop, then walk away. Practice ways to ignore the hurtful remarks, like acting uninterested.

• **REPORT ONLINE BULLYING**, such as abusive posts on social media platforms.

• **TELL AN ADULT**—parents, teachers, and other adults at school can all help stop bullying.

DISCRIMINATION

Discrimination means treating a person unfairly because of who they are, and is often related to RACE, GENDER, CLASS, SEXUALITY, NATIONALITY, BEHAVIOR, APPEARANCE, AGE, CULTURE, ABILITY, or IDENTITY. Discrimination can have a huge impact on mental health.

Discrimination comes in many forms but commonly includes actions such as: being excluded, people saying hurtful things to you, and people treating you differently because they think you are "different." It's important to remember that you don't have to be like anyone else. Don't follow the crowd just because you feel you should.

RESTORING CONFIDENCE

Dealing with bullying and discrimination can make you feel less confident and zap your energy. It can be hard to keep positive but it is vital to remember that you are not at fault. To rebuild your confidence, try:

- Spending time with people who love you
- Being creative
- Keeping active
- Taking a break from social media
- Writing down your good points
- Finding one positive thing each day
- Relaxing.

WE ARE ALL DIFFERENT AND THIS IS SOMETHING TO CELEBRATE!

BEING YOU

In all the world there is nobody quite like you! There are people who are different and people who are similar, but nobody is exactly the same, with the same thoughts, ideas, feelings, behaviors, dreams, words, hopes, fantasies, and appearance.

YOU ARE UNIQUE!

This is not about pretending that we are perfect and have perfect lives! It's about recognizing our strengths and unique qualities so we can build on them and become stronger and more resilient.

Self-esteem

Self-esteem is the opinion we have of ourselves. When we have healthy self-esteem, we feel positive about ourselves and about life in general. When we have low self-esteem, we see ourselves in a more negative and critical light. Some days we will feel happy to be who we are. Other days less so. Sometimes we will need to work harder to feel good about ourselves and this is **NORMAL**.

YOU DO YOU!

1.
Spend time with people who like you and care about you.

2.
Ignore and stay away from people who put you down or treat you badly.

3.
Do things that you enjoy.

4.
Do things that make you feel good.

5.
Do things you are good at.

6.
Reward yourself for your successes.

7.
Develop your talents and skills.

8.
Be your own best friend and treat yourself well.

9.
Make choices for yourself and don't let others make those choices for you.

10.
Take responsibility for yourself, your choices, and your actions.

11.
Always do what you believe is right.

12.
Be true to yourself and your values.

13.
Respect other people and treat them well.

14.
Set goals and work to achieve them.

15.
Don't beat yourself up when you get it wrong.

STOP, THINK, & REFLECT

How do you feel about yourself right now? It may be helpful to discuss your thoughts and the ideas above with a trusted adult or friend. Is there anything else that you can do to boost your personal positivity?

SUPPORT NETWORKS

We all need support to help keep us in good mental health and to manage life's ups and downs. Needing support is not a weakness—being able to find and accept support from those who care about us is a strength. We can learn from them and we feel safe when they care for us. Never be afraid to ask for help.

YOUR ENERGIZERS

It's important to recognize your energizers. These are the people you feel happiest with. When you leave them at the end of a visit or chat you feel energized. They say and do things to make you feel good. Who are your energizers? Talking to these people and thinking about some of the positive things they have said and done for you might help next time you feel low.

CIRCLE OF SUPPORT

As well as your energizers, think about ALL of the people who can support you and that you trust. These people form your circle of support—your team. Together, they form a network of people you can rely on.

TRY THIS ACTIVITY TO RECORD YOUR CIRCLE OF SUPPORT SO THAT YOU CAN SEE IT, FEEL IT, AND USE IT IF YOU NEED A REMINDER OF THE PEOPLE YOU ARE CONNECTED TO.

1. Draw a big circle on a piece of paper.

2. Write your name in the middle.

3. Write down all the people you could turn to for support around your name. For example: family, friends, teachers, doctors, and counselors.

Spending time outdoors, especially in green spaces, is a great way to boost your mental health and happiness.

THE POWER OF NATURE

You might not always feel like going outdoors, especially if your mood is low, but stepping outside can give your mind a moment of peace. Look around you, connect with the surroundings, and awaken your senses. What can you see? What can you hear? What can you feel? What can you smell?

You don't have to live in the countryside to experience the power of nature—your garden, city parks, or even just taking a walk down the street can give you time and space to breathe.

GROWING GREEN

Growing or caring for a plant can be a great way to connect with nature. Looking after it and watching its progress as it develops can be really uplifting and make you feel good about yourself. Why not try planting some seeds and giving it a try? You don't even need to have an outdoor space—you can grow house plants and herbs inside, bringing nature to you.

HELPING OTHERS

Part of being a mentally fit person is being able to make and keep positive relationships with others, by supporting them and taking care of them when they have difficulties, and celebrating with them when they have successes. It's about sharing both happy and sad times together.

BUILDING EMPATHY

Empathy is the ability to understand and share the feelings of another. It can sometimes be difficult to see another person's point of view, especially when our own emotions are triggered. This is because our emotions work faster than our thinking and interpreting skills. Showing empathy requires the ability to recognize and respond to someone else's emotions.

MIND READING

It's not always easy to detect what someone else is feeling. None of us can mind read, but there are some signals and signs we can look for. Ask yourself:

- What does the person look like?

- What does their facial expression suggest?

- What words are they using?

- What tone of voice are they using?

- How are they moving and walking?

Think about what the person is doing right now and compare it to how they usually are or have been in the past. Do you notice any differences? These changes might be a clue to how they are feeling.

Helping others who are suffering

If you know a friend is feeling sad or stressed there are some things you can do to help. Before you jump in, here are some guidelines to bear in mind:

• Make time to be with them and just listen. Find somewhere to go that is peaceful, without distractions.

• Let them tell you as much as they want, but don't pressure them to open up. Talking can take a lot of trust and courage. You may be the first person they have felt able to talk to.

• Don't try to be an expert. Listen and think before you give advice, otherwise you may jump to the wrong conclusion.

• Discuss ways of coping, such as exercise, relaxation, and challenging negative thoughts.

• Listen carefully to what they tell you and repeat what they have said back to them to make sure you have understood it.

• Offer to go with them to talk to a trusted adult or doctor if more help is required.

• Don't try to be the one who saves them—know your limits! If you think your friend is in danger or may hurt themselves, you must take action to make sure they are safe. This might include calling a helpline (see page 63) or telling an adult right away.

BEING WELL AND STAYING WELL

It can be easier to make changes and keep improving our mental health if we make a wellbeing plan and set ourselves goals for the future.

Your wellbeing toolbox

This book includes lots of different tools and strategies for protecting your mental health. You may find that some work better than others. You may even have your own. This is fine. Everyone needs to develop their own wellbeing toolbox, filled with the tools and strategies that work for **YOU**. It's also key to keep thinking about how you can build upon these ideas or change them when you need to. Remember your favorite tools and strategies and try to make time for them to help you live a happy and healthy life.

KEYS TO EMOTIONAL WELLBEING

When making plans and goals, try to remember and focus on these key aspects of wellbeing:

Connect
Make an effort to be social and connect with others.

Be active
Exercise improves both your physical and mental health.

Keep learning
What do you know today that you did not know yesterday?

Give
Be kind and give to others.

Be mindful
Focus on the moment and enjoy the here and now.

PLANNING FOR WELLBEING

Start by thinking about the **KEYS TO EMOTIONAL WELLBEING**. Write down ideas for actions and activities you could do to include each of the keys in your life. Aim to do one action per key, each day. You could use a whiteboard to plan your daily actions or start a wellbeing planner in a notebook. Remember that it's only a plan—don't feel like you've failed if you don't manage everything on the list!

MENTAL HEALTH GOALS

Setting realistic goals can be a great way to boost mental health. Having something to focus on can take your mind off worries and achieving a goal can make you feel positive and proud. Why not try setting goals for each of the keys to emotional wellbeing. Make sure your goals are **SMART**:

Specific—e.g. I will be active every day.

Measurable—e.g. I will jog around the park every day, for 30 minutes.

Achievable—e.g. I have time after school and my friend has agreed to jog with me.

Realistic and Relevant—e.g. keeping active will improve my physical and mental health.

Time-limited—e.g. I will try this during the summer term.

...and finally, set a date when you will review your goals with someone who is important to you and who has your best interests at heart.

Good luck and
GO FOR IT!

CONCLUSION

As well as increasing awareness of common mental health conditions such as anxiety and depression, by reading this book you will hopefully have picked up some tips, tricks, and ideas to boost your mental health and understand what keeps it healthy.

Remember that happiness is a journey! It's all about learning to cope with life's ups and downs, and remembering to be kind by supporting each other—especially those who are finding life hard.

We also need to be kind to ourselves! Look after you. **YOU ARE ENOUGH** and you should never let anyone say otherwise. Keep your thinking positive, recognize and build on your strengths, and challenge negative thoughts. Keep trying to be OK every day, and don't give up.

AUTHOR'S NOTE

As a Positive Psychologist, I feel very strongly that we can ALL do more to look after our mental health and that we are ALL capable of being happier on a daily basis. I've worked with children and young people throughout my career, which has spanned well over 30 years. Through my work and research, I look at strengths, what builds these in people, and what makes them happier and more able to lead meaningful lives.

I hope that you find this book useful and enjoy working through it. I have included lots of ideas and strategies that I have seen work—for many children and young people but also for me, too! My belief is that we all need to nurture our wellbeing, and that being able to do so is one of life's challenges—and one that is best tackled together.

Dr. Tina Rae
Writer and Psychologist

NOTES FOR PARENTS,

Mental wellbeing is important for everyone, but it's especially important for children and young people. Good mental health allows them to develop resilience and grow into well-rounded, healthy adults.

Here are some ways in which we can help children manage stress and anxiety, as well as some more general tips for supporting mental health:

• **Listen, watch, and notice.** Being aware of how a child is acting, thinking, and feeling can help you pick up on low mood, as well as early signs of more serious mental health conditions, such as depression. Pay extra attention during times of change.

• **Encourage children to talk about how they feel** and provide opportunities for them to voice their concerns. Try to use open questions like "why don't you tell me how you're feeling?" rather than saying "I can see you're stressed."

• **Don't be afraid of talking about mental health.** Aim to increase awareness, encourage dialogue, reduce stigma, and develop understanding.

• **Be wary of telling a child to "pull yourself together," or that something is "nothing to worry about."** Sometimes, unhappiness is more serious than it may seem on the surface.

• **Aim to lead by example**—exercise, eat heathily, have screen-free time every day, use mindfulness, maintain a positive mental attitude, practice relaxation, and show that self-care isn't selfish.

• **Help children to face the things or situations they fear.** Learning to face fears is one of the most challenging parts of overcoming anxiety and stress. Facing fears usually works best if tackled gradually, one step at a time.

• **Encourage exercise.** For children who are less keen on sports, try something you can do together, such as yoga, a bike ride, or a walk in the park.

• **Take bullying and discrimination seriously.** Talk to your child, look out for signs, and offer support. Consider having a discussion with your child's school if an issue needs to be escalated.

• **Try some acts of kindness together.** Bake cakes for neighbors, donate old clothes to charity, or volunteer at a local event to show that being kind can have a positive impact.

• **Encourage online safety.** Check, assess, and adjust parental locks if necessary.

GUARDIANS, AND TEACHERS

- **Try to manage your own anxiety** and show young people that it can be managed. Share your strategies so that children can try them, too.

- **Balance reassurance with new ideas.** When a child comes to you with something they are worried about, listen and try to understand what is happening. Offer reassurance and explore with them what they could do to manage their fears. During the process, check in to see what is working well and what isn't, then discuss alternative options, if required.

- **Support children to challenge negative or irrational beliefs and thoughts.** Model and communicate effective ways to question and challenge anxiety provoking thoughts and beliefs.

- **Be calm and patient.** Sometimes, behaviors of anxious children may seem unreasonable. It's important to remember that an anxious young person who cries or avoids situations is, in fact, responding instinctively to a perceived threat.

- **Support children to accept uncertainty and cope with change.** Talk about outcomes and aim to help children embrace and deal with both positive and negative change.

- **Make sure children know they can come to you for help and support.** Also remind them that there are other people who can give more specific help, if you need to tackle a more serious problem together. Knowing that they can call on others for support can reduce anxiety.

- **Be honest (up to a point!) with children about your own feelings.** Use your discretion, but sharing how you feel can encourage children to do the same. Communication can help to reduce misunderstandings and avoid thoughts and feelings being bottled up inside.

- **Encourage healthy sleeping patterns** and a regular bedtime to help children stay fit and well.

- **Remember that no one is perfect** and people get things wrong sometimes. Even you!

FURTHER RESOURCES

APPS

Calm Harm
An app designed to help people resist or manage the urge to self-harm.

Catch It
Catch It helps users learn how to manage feelings like anxiety and depression, and better understand their moods through use of an ongoing diary.

Clear Fear
An app to help with managing anxiety, reducing physical responses to threat, and changing thoughts and behaviors.

distrACT
An app that provides information and advice about self-harm and suicidal thoughts.

For Me
An app from Childline offering advice, counseling and group message boards.

MeeTwo
An app to help teenagers talk about difficult things, with a safe and secure forum for teenagers wanting to discuss any issue affecting their lives.

MindShift
An app with advice for relaxation methods and managing anxiety.

Recharge—Move Well, Sleep Well, Be Well
A personalized six-week program to help improve mood and energy levels.

SAM
SAM (Self-help for Anxiety Management) has games and tools to help users understand and manage anxiety.

Smiling Mind
Mindfulness meditations aimed at reducing stress and anxiety, and boosting concentration levels.

Stress & Anxiety Companion
On-the-go support for stress and anxiety, providing tools like breathing exercises, relaxing music and games.

The publishers and author cannot be held responsible for the content of the apps and websites referred to in this book. All web addresses were correct at the time of printing.

WEBSITES AND HELPLINES

Change Grow Live
www.changegrowlive.org
Help and advice about drug or alcohol issues.

CMHN
www.cmhnetwork.org
The Children's Mental Health Network (CMHN) provides services, information, ideas, and solutions for children with mental health needs and their families.

Kooth
www.kooth.com
Free, safe, and anonymous online mental wellbeing community for young people.

LGBT National Help Center
www.glbthotline.org
National Youth Talkline: 1-800-246-7743
The Lesbian, Gay, Bisexual, and Transgender (LGBT) National Help Center provides peer-support, community connections, and information for people with questions regarding sexual orientation and/or gender identity. The hotline and chat service provide help with things like coming-out issues, safer-sex information, school bullying, family concerns, and relationship problems.

NAMI
www.nami.org
1-800-950-6264
The National Alliance on Mental Illness (NAMI) is a mental health organization dedicated to building better lives for the millions of Americans affected by mental illness. NAMI offers a helpline, a video resource library, online discussion groups, and general information about mental health.

NEDA
www.nationaleatingdisorders.org
(800) 931-2237
The National Eating Disorders Association (NEDA) is dedicated to supporting individuals and families affected by eating disorders. Contact the helpline, chat or text service for support, resources, and treatment options for yourself or a loved one.

OCD Youth
www.ocdyouth.org
Support for young people with obsessive compulsive disorder, including e-helpline.

Pacer's National Bullying Prevention Center
www.pacer.org/bullying/
PACER provides innovative resources for students, parents, educators, and others, and recognizes bullying as a serious community issue that impacts education, physical, and emotional health, and the safety and well-being of students.

SAMHSA
www.samhsa.gov/find-treatment
The Substance Abuse and Mental Health Services Administration (SAMHSA) aims to reduce the impact of substance abuse and mental illness on America's communities. The helpline provides confidential advice, treatment referrals, and information for individuals and families facing mental and/or substance use disorders.

Teen Mental Health.org
www.teenmentalhealth.org
Teen Mental Health.org provides information and resources for young people, families, educators, community agencies, and health care providers. These materials are provided in a variety of mediums, including videos, animations, brochures, e-books, and online training programs.

INDEX